AF506714

This is not your grandmother's Ramadan collection—this a collection for all the moonstruck girlies in the back rows of the musalla fighting for our lives!

— Sagirah Shahid, writer, educator, performance artist

*

In *Grasping at This Planet Just to Believe*, Tanzila Ahmed's inspired and inspiring new collection, the speaker declares, "In my truth, / faith / is sung / with love." It's this love that gives these poems so much power, beauty, tenderness, bite, and luminosity. To be Muslim in America, Ahmed reminds us, is in itself a daily practice of defiance and vigilance, of self-discovery and self-love, especially when one is Brown, a woman, and an activist. To survive and thrive, one must be in solidarity with others, and these poems—all composed during ten years of Poem-a-Day for Ramadan, an inclusive, multifaith online community which Ahmed founded—speak to just how effectively poetry can help us bear witness to one another's struggles related to illness, grief, and victimization, as well as to our collective triumphs, joys, and healing journeys. This book shows us how "Ramadan is about empathy, and giving, and the humanity of all," and invites readers to share in its generous energy too.

— Faisal Mohyuddin, author of *Elsewhere: An Elegy*

*

I laughed and cried and got goosebumps more than once! Every one of Taz's poems hit a spiritual nerve and together this collection makes up an incredibly comforting and uplifting companion for seekers—both in and out of Ramadan.

— Edina Lekovic, creator of L.A. Muslim History

A bubbling cauldron of poetry exploring pleasure, grief, &
healing. Taz's words sing especially bright when sharing the
evolution of her grief in the wake of her beloved mother's death;
and in her exploration of the jasmine & jacaranda legacies of her
Bangladeshi family, American home, and chosen Muslim family.

— Ayesha Mattu, editor of "Love, InshAllah: The Secret Love
Lives of American Muslim Women" and "Salaam, Love: American
Muslim Men on Love, Sex & Intimacy"

*

Tanzila Ahmed's *Grasping at This Planet Just to Believe* enacts
a poetic attention which she invites to change her. It's work I'm
deeply grateful for, and I feel changed. Changed by poems that
witness and resist, by a revelatory poet who offers talisman and
prayer, storytelling, wholiness, and love: outward and inward.
Through difficulties and violence, with received and made
traditions, she holds the names of her beloveds, in all their
forms, with a poet's defiant and yearning faith.

Read this book, let Ahmed equip you "with enough love and fire
to face this grief filled unjust world as fighters and with bravado.
Ameen."

— Hari Alluri, author of *The Flayed City*

*

Tanzila Ahmed writes at the intersections of spirituality, grief,
community, and ritual—inspired by the many moons and
phases of Ramadan. With this collection, Ahmed invites us
into her singular experience—seeped in LA sunsets and Spring
wildflowers, Eid wishes and midnight contemplations about
what it means to be a Muslim woman, artist and activist in these
harrowing times.

— Neelanjana Banerjee, Kaya Press

Tanzila's poetry is a window into the personal threshold where deep grief, loss of belief, memory, gritty cities, mystical visions, faith and the unseen exist all at once.

In *Grasping at This Planet Just to Believe*, Taz unveils the the inner dimensions of a deep and private devotion and prayer for a lost beloved. Through her words, we move alongside her, near and around the city of angels, touching up at boom boxes, candy skies, sharp memories, doctors words...at last into our own dedicate longing.

— Fariba Alam, artist

*

When I discuss Taz Ahmed and her work, I always mention the same thing: she is the queen of community building. Her sense of justice and her organizing principles have informed her writing and network since I first encountered her as a blogger on Sepia Mutiny. At this stage in her career, many people would go inwards, but Taz is always scaffolding outward. This latest collection of tender, nostalgic poems written in online community during Ramadan is the latest example of a commitment to always striving for better for us all.

— Ahmed Ali Akbar, host of *See Something Say Something*

Grasping at This Planet Just to Believe

Poetry a Day Over a Decade of Ramadans

by Tanzila Ahmed

table of contents

Introduction to *Grasping at This Planet Just to Believe*

In the Muslim tradition, fasting is not meant to a "mortification of the flesh," as it is in the Christian tradition, nor is it meant as an "atonement," as it is in the Jewish tradition. Rather, it follows similar ascetic practices of South Asian religions in that it is a practice unto itself, perhaps as a preparation to receive benefits. Like exercise, fasting uses actions of the body itself to learn more about existence. In this sense, a Muslim practitioner does not deny the body in order to achieve spiritual knowledge—i.e. material physical carnal existence is not meant to be "transcended" by some kind of "higher" understanding. One who fasts is one who honors the body and its processes.

There is another way that fasting in the Muslim tradition is very different than fasting in other traditions: it is both sustained—repeated over an entire lunar cycle—and also not tied to incidents, i.e. one does not fast for any specific purpose or ceremonial moment. While it is true that the Night of Majesty, called Lail-at-al-Qadr in Arabic, happens during the month of Ramadan, it is not a focal point of the fasting. Certain prayers and rituals happen on that night and the ones around it, but fasting happens before, during, and after the Night. And many Muslims who fast celebrate it in different ways. It is not even a fixed point: because there is disagreement about which night it is, rituals are performed on three separate nights. For some Muslims, the beginning and end of the month also are not fixed in time but depend on the sighting of the earliest sliver of a waxing crescent. The month hasn't begun until it is sighted; it has not ended until the next one is similarly sighted. As fasting is a practice, so too did Tanzila Ahmed make of her own writing a practice. As fasting is most beneficially a community practice, so too did she make of her own writing a community practice, sharing space and time with others, building a community where none was before. For Taz, the community aspect was paramount—if writers did not regularly share their work they were removed from the group! It meant that the community was intentional, that the writers in it were not only committed to the practices of fasting and writing, but they were committed to supporting the community in both endeavors by sharing their own work.

One doesn't think of fasting and writing as separate practices in the reading of *Grasping At the Planet Just to Believe*. Rather one sees how the bodily of practice of fasting—withdrawing from food and drink during daylight hours—helps to focus sensory perceptions and the mind's attention, resulting in poems that are very much informed by the physical conditions in which they were created.

When I edited the anthology *New Moons: Contemporary Writing by North American Muslims*, I knew how important it was to include Muslims of all kinds. For too long, the Muslim ummah has been defined both from within and without as too narrow, to exclusionary. The truth of the matter is that the ummah is diverse, inclusive, and powerful because of its plurality. Taz worked hard to make sure that all were welcome in her community—religious Muslims, cultural Muslims, feminists, secular Muslims— as well as all different kinds of writers from varying experiences.

The poems in the book itself—drawn from over ten years of writing—speak to this range of interests. They interrogate received spiritual and religious ideas, they celebrate the beauty of the world and the humans that live in it, they imagine futures of justice and equality. Populated by a profusion of flowers and resounding with birdsong and the echoing call to prayer, these poems are first and foremost PRAISE, an action that feels radical and radically compassionate in this conflicted world we find ourselves in.

Following the cycles of the moon in its structure, as does the month of Ramadan itself, this book is an essential testament to the ways a spiritual life and a physical life are not separate from one another but one unified lived experience. "Wisdom is there on the edge," she writes, "and we are halfway there." Taz Ahmed has made a beautiful book and I am grateful to her for it.

— Kazim Ali,
author of *Fasting for Ramadan: Notes on a Spiritual Practice*

PROLOGUE

Every Ramadan since my mother's passing, I've written daily poems as a practice of prayer during the month of Ramadan. Daily poems, over one lunar month over ten years. 2,800 poems, if I had actually done it without fail. Some years were more successful than others, depending on the year, the season, the heart, the world politics, the grief. Some years, all I did was write two poems and then fall into a depth of nothingness.

Ramadan is the holy month of Islam, where Muslim around the world fast from food, abstain from 'bad' behaviors, and re-commit themselves to prayers. It's often considered a spiritual re-set with the fasting from food giving a sense of clarity. In a world where reality is so often a distraction, Ramadan feels like a deliberate annual reminder of Allah and faith and love in this world.

Poetry has always been a way for me to process the jumbled up feelings I had in this confusing world. When I was writing poems, I was able to interact with my feelings, and process reality. I started writing poems for Ramadan to heal from grief by giving myself the discipline of practicing art. It helped – fasting helped, but writing about what I was experiencing while I was fasting helped me connect in a way that prayer never was able to. I was taught dogmatic prayers – reciting Arabic words that I didn't understand. But poetry was my words. As the years went on, I stopped being able to fast for a variety of health reason and through poetry I was able to still foster a Ramadan spiritualty without fasting.

In the past ten years, this practice has grown as I invited friends to join me. Every year, I collected more and more writers into a Facebook group where people were encouraged to write daily, share once a week, and if they didn't share or intro selves, they were booted. Each person needed to have a real world connection to someone. I was wary of informants and creepy lurkers, and wanted to create a safe space for Muslim and Muslim-ish people to express themselves fully without fear of surveillance. After each Ramadan, I hosted an Eid Poetry reading in Los Angeles featuring the poets in this group.

I read every Ramadan poem posted in the group. As the moderator of the space, it was my form of accountability, to confirm to them that their words had a witness. I invited Muslims on the margins who no longer felt welcome in conservative Muslim spaces. I invited hijabi women whose poetry were more duas than prose. I invited people who were allies to Muslims and were already in community with us. There were artists who drew, or photographed or wrote songs or watercolored daily. There were published bestselling poets and amateur writers. There were people who never saw themselves as poets who wrote in the space and later would publish the poems they wrote. We presented on panels at various writer conferences, like Association of Writers and Writing Programs and Thinking Its Presence; and performed from bookstores to mosques. Deep friendships were made with people who we only spoke with online.

In the past decade we've seen an incredible amping up of islamophobia in America. What first started out as 9/11 backlash a decade later had morphed into the systematization of hate against Muslims for political gain in white supremacy. This has turned the month of Ramadan often into the most violent time of the year for Muslims where hate crimes run rampant and mosques are attacked with more ferocity. In turn, the poems written became a collective place of trauma reflection and communal healing.

This project has become one of the most spiritually fulfilling part of how I connect to the world during Ramadan. I hope these poems can support you on your journey as well.

— Tanzila "Taz" Ahmed

*Dedicated to the Poetry-A-Day for Ramadan crew
and to our insistence in creating a Third Space
for us to pray together.*

بِسْمِ اللهِ الرَّحْمٰنِ الرَّحِيمِ

NEW MOON
CHAPTER 1

The first day of Ramadan is marked by the sighting of the new moon.

THE MOON

Look at the moon.
Is she there yet?
Do you know her like that?
How she smiles and shines and wanes through the sky?
Can you feel her glances, even when you can't see her?
When she enters the universe
how everyone stops
to find her in the sky?
She is new.
She should be.
But tell me
Is she here?

WISHING

What if zamzam water was really magic?
And prayer rugs could fly high?
I would then grant you one wish -
Not the kind of wish from rubbing a brass lamp
or catching a flying jinn by her hair.
It would be more like
the blessing from seeing the green flash at Maghreb time
or catching a leaf in your open hand under a tree.
It wouldn't be an impossible wish.
I can't take you soaring on horseback through the seven
heavens
or hide you in secret caves behind spider webs.
It would be a gentler wish
like forgiveness
or forgetting
or starting over.
I'd grant you the wish to never feel pain
or to fall in love and to feel loved
or to never feel afraid to exist wholly in your skin.
I am no angel
But in a world of miracles and cross-dimensional whispers
if I could
I'd grant you
this
one
wish.

ORANGE

I want to fill your mouth
with marigolds
till they cascade down
unraveling into a glorious carpet
that I can fall backwards on
and stuff my mouth full.

JACARANDAS & JASMINES

Jacarandas and jasmines
back-lit by June gloom
is Los Angeles' current mood.
Late-to-blossom purple sappy flowers
stick to sandals underfoot.
Evenings are scented intoxicatingly
from the white night-blooming stars.
The romance of spring
gets smothered in the morning gloom.
It is the season of what could have been
if left to be.
Rejections before initiation
regrets you didn't have the chance to make.
Nipped buds falling to the ground
weeds cracking sidewalks pulled out by the roots
green leaves falling before turning –
this lonely never had a chance.
Soon, will come summer and heat,
Sweaty lust and hot crush.
Maybe forever love.
But for now,
it's just jacarandas, jasmines,
and June glooms
catching us unaware
another year, once again.

CRYSTALIZED

at night I cuddle rocks when I sleep
citrine and tiger eye held to my belly to drive fear from gut
on my nightstand sits a purple amethyst to keep insomnia
at bay
under my bed a cup of water to capture my bad dreams
rose quartz tumble to my feet when I take off my bra
held close to my heart to un-break it
in my pockets smoky quartz to ground me in place
no matter where I travel on this earth
my fingers are ringed like the Beloved's aqeeq –
a Sri Lankan opal, a Nepalese aquamarine, a fortuitous
moonstone,
a green agate to protect against negativity –
a rock collection scratching at the surface.
in the cave of my chest crystals grow from saltwater tears
belly full of rocks weighing me down
clenched fists smash
head to ground
sometimes, I am grasping at this planet just to believe

BIRTHDAY

In the glorious
bright pink streaky sunset
I almost forgot her.
So she
showed herself
to me.
Of course she
would appear at Maghreb time
blanketing the prairie
her birthday
Ramadan's first day
a kismet of a coincidence.
How does grief ebb like that?
Memory shadows faded
until my sister's graveside photo
reminded me I was supposed to be sad today
I am not sad today.
I don't want to forget.
But how else do I remember.

POPPIES

Inspired by Nina Simone's 'Poppies'

We took selfies
in the orange meadows
amongst the flowers of forgetfulness
claiming our presence brashly
insisting that we three sisters
will be seen
in colorful beauty and joy.
Despite what they told me.

We skipped on trails
while rattlesnakes slithered
hidden within the field of poppies.
Were we the petals or the prey?
Take a deep breath
if you are reaching for truth
and avoid a poisoned nap on the way
to see the wizard.
Three sisters awoke
demanding to not forget.

FLOWERS ARE BACK

The first jacarandas are in bloom
        I saw my first today
            the lilac blush
of the new jacarandas' buds
reminded me of how they remind me of Neelanjana
and how she drives around Los Angeles seeking these blooms
until I gave them to her as a birthday gift
so she'd never have to seek again.

The way that
        now
            the heady smell
of the night blossoming jasmines
reminds me of how Ammu used to keep
a small bowl of water with blooms
by her bedside because they reminded her of home
so now I keep a dying plant on my balcony
in hopes I can smell when she visits my dreams.

The way that
        whenever
            the white fragrant blossoms
turn into round oranges on trees
remind me of how the steps up to Navneet's door
squish in summers with juice
before being comforted by her house
        so that friend-love always feels a bit squishy.

The way that
        in the summer
            the ripe hot pink prickly pears
                lining along the flat spray of cactus

will remind me of that one summer of
escaping Kirin out of her hospital room and how
the brightness of the fruit looks like the ultrasound
looking inside her heart.

The way that when I pet the lavender
          I remember how Jenn and I went picking lavender
bundles
in the hills of Santa Cruz, just days after burying my
mother.

The way that from now on out when I see fields of orange
poppies
          I will forever remember the road trip
with my sisters to Antelope Valley
singing about the Wizard of Oz and wondering
who would make it snow for us.

How bright pink azaleas
reminds me of being a pre-teen running away from our
home
in the desert of Saudi Arabia and straight to my best
friend's home.

How I plucked honeysuckles
as a kid with my friends and ran my tongue along the
stamen
for hint of sweetness.

How we pluck petals asking for love
how these petals fall in paths
how we eat the fruit from the blooms
worms and all.

SPRING IN MY DREAMS

I dreamt the jacarandas were in bloom last night.
I am charmed by the love letters in my nightmares.
The petals dissolved into vermin in outstretched fingers.
I woke to etiolated succulents and yellow-leaved pothos.
My perennials struggle to be alive - all on the path for slow suicide.
The scents of car pollution and night blooming jasmine lull me to sleep.
I wait for the sticky sap of the jacaranda flowers to fall in my dreams.

FLOWERS FOR NEELANJANA

While searching for a fence of fuchsia bougainvillea
I find you a pine trunk covered in a white wall of blooming
jasmines.
We are surprised into a nostalgia of a motherland that was
never ours.

Let's play hooky and pretend that these graffiti-ed L.A.
streets
are really the wet rice paddy fields of Bengal.
Carefree and wild, we will tell golpos while sitting on the
mathi and braiding jasmine stars into each other's junglee
wild hair.
I would have strung a curtain of white flowers for your
bridal bed and you would have spread petals on mine
In these Bengalese worlds.

Every time I see a jacaranda tree in full violet sappy bloom
here in springtime Los Angeles
I am reminded of your love for your son
and how you drive him around on these concrete streets in
search of these sticky blooms.
His future nostalgia.
Jasmine always reminds me of this kind of love for my own
mother.
With a moment of scent, I can pretend like she never left.

It's time to play hooky - the white jasmines, violet
jacarandas, and fuchsia bougainvillea are in bloom.

MORNING CALL

A very loud bird woke me up at 6am
singing outside my window
like fajr azaan.
Nature's trickery has no bounds.
Blessings and miracles
I mean.

ENFLOWERED JUMMAH

Our pre-Ramadan preparations involved a Jummah
frolicking in the beautiful tulips, camelias, wisterias while
glorifying the beauty we saw in one another.
We prayed.
In tree shade, sun specked, pollen mist, perfumed clouds,
we prayed.
Tulips pink with soft spike rimmed faces and
intensely velvety purple petals begged to be petted.
We dipped our nose deeply in lilac bushes inhaling all of
Allah's glory.
We kneeled in the green grass, dirt clinging, and
closed our eyes to the sun, skin flushing, submitting to
nature.
We praised each other like we were praising the Almighty,
because Her Love exists in all of us and
your existence is proof of Her Love.

Through our camera lens we instrumented our bodies like
a blessed mirror revealing a love in one another
we couldn't truly see in ourselves.
Our photos exclaimed,
"Your beauty is Nature's beauty is Allah's beauty,
here is the proof embossed in flora, forever."
This Jummah was photogenic.
Stand in the flowers and be pretty
– this is your natural state of stunning.
You are gorgeous.
The old couple sat on a bench and looked on at us smiling
as we laughed and skipped amongst
azaleas and roses and cherry blossoms.
They smiled at our silly joy.

We primped and posed
with smiles on our faces.

May we always be mirrors for each other
that we are each natures' miracle, Allah's love.
Glory be.
Ameen.

WAXING CRESCENT
CHAPTER 2

The first ten days of Ramadan are the days of Mercy and Blessing.

WE MAKE OUR OWN TRADITIONS

I drove alone to the Desert Oasis dodging butterflies
and tumbleweeds to only find the store had closed at 4
pm I didn't know oases had closing times. The tall palms
overhead let streaks of sun shine through and dates palms
for acres and acres lined up in rows. I drove through the
desert again, racing against closing time of another oasis,
this one closing at 5 p.m. I taste tested Barhi, Deglet Noor,
and Zahidis before I found what I was looking for – the
soft mushy Medjools. *Do desert jinns attach themselves to
boxes of dates to be taken home for Ramadan iftars across
California?* I wondered. A box of Ramadan dates, check.
A meal at the King's Highway, check. A date milkshake,
check. We must fight to make our own traditions even
when alone, even when society tells us our people like us
are worth less than the rest. So, I grasp at palm dates and
shake trees until the dates are all mine. I drive back West
under the moonless desert sky with a trunk full of dates
– is this Ramadan tradition actually a tradition, even if it's
just for one all alone?

FIRST HUNGER, SECOND TASTE

I still tasted him lingering on my lips
after our midnight car kiss
the night before the first fast of Ramadan.
My tongue thirsted
I hungered
wudu would not wash away his bite
I spent all day
wondering if my mouth was bit or my lips were licked
if it would break my fast
for how he lingered.
All day I hungered for nothing else.

WHICH WAY TO PRAY

The time of the year to
re-string the thosbee beads broken off in rearview mirrors
wash the headscarves with old sweat stains
dust the turquoise threadbare prayer rug
and figure out which direction
Mecca is again, this year
even though the direction to pray never changes
but in a directionless life
where time passes by measures of grief
or casual flings or Costco cards
and where all roads lose into themselves
it all feels infinitely arbitrary
Maybe this will be
the year reset will stick
I'll know from my soul
which way to face
And I'll remember
to not forget
again.

IS IT TIME?

Dancing under the shadow of the dark side of the moon
squinted eyes
through dupatta gauze and
between clouds on mountaintops
we turn to the sky for answers.
For time.
For forgiveness.
Trying to catch a glimpse of the flash
of heavens gates opening
telling us, again,
it has arrived.
It is time.
Open dua-ed hands raise skyward
let the tears rain down.

RAMADAN RITUALS

Sage the apartment from corner to floor.
Dust off the blue prayer mat.
Carry three juicy dates in a Ziploc bag at all times.
Look deep to the sky for the new moon.
Download the Ramadan app for your phone.
Eat Frosted Flakes for suhoor.
Clutch the thosbees you wear around your wrist.
Say Bismillah.
Read your star sign daily.
Take your shoes off at the door and hang them from the
power lines.
Whisper spells and suras and manifestations.
Wrap a scarf around your neck that doubles as hijab, as
needed.
Eat pistachio flavored frozen yogurt with cookie dough
after tarawih prayer.
Wear an amulet Allah necklace around your neck.
Make a wish setting your intentions.
Practice celibacy.
Make sure your mustard oil is fresh.
Light a Guadalupe jar candle nightly for those not home.
Leave the porch light on outside for Dad
for when he comes home from the mosque.
Get an iftar to-go box from Little Bangladesh to eat in your
car.
Water your plants – don't forget because you can't drink
water yourself.
Take a nap.
Ground yourself by sinking deeply into the earth, then
breathe.
Do not say that you are hungry or thirsty.
Gaze at the moon through a gauzy dupatta for a ring.

Ignore the judgmental auntie stares when in Artesia
shopping for an Eid outfit.
Pay zakat online to your favorite Muslim civil rights group.
Pull out $10 cash from the bank to pay for parking at Eid
prayer.
Roll roshogullahs so tight that they squeak when eaten.
Paint henna on your hands then fall asleep open handed.
Pray on plastic in a large suburban convention center.
Pour one out for the homies.
Lay flowers at the grave.
Cry.

MOON

The first night of Ramadan
and she, the crescent moon, smiles slyly off-kilter
like a devilish disappearing Cheshire cat
resting on the dark branch of the Milky Way
or an angelic man on the moon one-eyed winking.
A sliver of light in the sky finally sighted
she will wax till she wanes
watching these Ramadan nights
holding back the devils
while observing to see how the cookie crumbles.
Her shine foreshadows captious or rapturous
- depending on how you look at it -
this new moon in the night sky.
Anyways, she is to be our witness.

BIRDSONG

The first night of Ramadan
the mockingbird outside sings love songs from midnight
into suhoor
He sings loudly, a diverse repertoire
of every sound he's ever heard.
He mansplains us his lonesome and his territory
trilling to attract love
chirping in chest-out bravado
till the sun rise silences.
He keeps us humans from sleeping
his singing our all-night tarawih prayer
reminding us that the darkest hours of the Ramadan nights
are the brightest and loudest
a devotion meant to be sung out.
Sleep in the holy month is for suckers.
For the rest of Ramadan
the azaan for suhoor will come from the lovesick
mockingbird
singing in his tree until daybreak
every night.

RAMADAN EVE

Lost in tangled tides
magnetic field flies
my needle spins wildly out of control
counter/
clockwise
no one way to go.
She was my compass
pointing me due North
no -
make that due Northeast
in the direction of the Kabbah
she was my guiding star to Allah.

She, who taught me how to bow to the Almighty –
She, whose love was a million tawafs around my soul –
She, whose actions were my reminders of faith above all
else.

Her teachings formed remembrance of «la ilaha illallah» on
my lip
innately, incessantly, thoughtlessly
my muscles remembered these words
whispered them in a drone
as we buried her into the ground
her face tilted northeast
remembering nothing else no more.

And now it is Ramadan Eve
Or is it?
Because the sighting
of the New Moon
dictates when the month of fasting begins

but in my universe the almighty new moon soothsayer was
my mother
something having to do with looking at the sky through a
cheesecloth
something to do with the moon's double halo
something that said that the moon was indeed new.
Till now...
So now how...?

My Ramadan started two months ago, exactly.
My new moon came with a late-night call.
Because the ultimate fast
the most difficult sacrifice
is to live a life without your mother in it.
A fast from your guiding light.

I've never prayed so much and so hard in my life.

NARY A BARE HEAD

I found my father sitting on the floor and ironing crisp creases into his cream colored thopis. Crocheted, embroidered, cotton, and satin — he carefully folds them so the crease goes straight through the center. They are now stacked on the table by the front door and each night as he heads out to tarawih prayer, he'll stuff one in his pocket. In my mind I picture how he will pull it out of his pocket as he walks up to the mosque doors, quickly placing it on his head as he lines up for his nightly prayers. I wonder if all the men are particular about the creases in their thopis, or if it is just him. I don't remember seeing creases in thopis ever before.

By the end of Ramadan, he will have hidden the thopis in his car's sunglass holder, glove compartment, and side door pocket. We will find them in sofa creases, bathroom drawers and by the phone in the kitchen.

But for now, they are stacked high, crisp clean, folded over twice, by the front door.

MARBLE MOUTHED LIP SYNC

The suras roll around like marbles in my mouth
but spill out like broken shattered teeth like in a bad dream
falling on dusty prayer mats from right to left
scattered between pauses and emptiness and blankness.
This all had meant something, at one time.
I have now forgotten the words to pray.
So, I only pray when I can silently echo
the words from someone else's mouth
pretending like their words are mine
mimicking lips like I know what to say.
I stand behind, stand next to, I stand by,
hoping/praying their blessing will shed onto me
freeriding residual nur, for a fraction of light.
Left alone
my own duas silenced at
the base of my throat.

Pray for me
make dua for me
because I've forgotten
how to make dua for myself.

SIGNS

The doctor called
at Maghrib time
the first night of Ramadan
sunsetting my pipe dreams.
Is this my body rebelling
for not being used
how it was supposed to be?
Patience is a virtue,
but overrated in a pandemic.
When I asked for a sign
this wasn›t what it was supposed to be.

PRAY FOR ME

Should I soak my cervix in sacred zumzum water?
Or yoni steam with the smoke from bukhoor incense?
Seven-Day Dhikr whispering Al-Khaliq?
Place a selenite shard on my womb?
Is faith just magical realism in real life?
Because immunity feels as intangible as black magic and
viruses feel as visible as jinns and
stress as manageable as angels.

When we pray
we blindly believe.
We meditate
to manifest our dreams.
We trust
in the universe.
We bow
to the unseen.

Why not
at least try
to make
magic real.

RAMADAN PROPHECY

Muhammad?

I look up from my phone in the waiting room of the
doctor's office. I'm waiting for Abbu, whose body is so
toxic it is crystalizing. It's the first day of Ramadan. A tall
attractive brown-skinned man walks to the door where the
nurse had called him. I slyly notice no ring on his finger.
I wonder what Muhammad's ailment is as he walks back
to the seat across from me. He looked healthy to me.
Chiseled jawline, broad back, taut muscles on his legs and
arms, dark curls tousled just so. I wonder for a split second
if he's even real, or maybe he was symbolism in skin, a
Ramadan reminder from the All-Knowing that prophecy is
everywhere. I wonder if this is foreshadowing in reality, a
circle back starting. Or maybe it was a test of my Ramadan
celibacy and clean thought purity. I wonder what kind of a
Muslim pick up line you use in the doctor's office.

I'd say *thoba thoba*, but it's not like it matters anyways.
Anyways.

So, I wait and the crystals keep replicating.

THE WORLD IS THIRSTING

With stolen water we break our fast
quenching our parched throats
while parching the desert for our thirst.
We drink like the prophet did
breaking our fast simply and
with the essence of what
makes us human.
Water cannot be owned and neither can people
but human bodies are 60% water
and we are shackled constantly.

They steal our rain to sell it back to us in plastic bottles
they poison the aquifers that belong to everyone
they drain us for almonds till we drought.
Lead bullets lace the water of Flint.
Water protectors battle bulldozers of Standing Rock.
Lakebeds are turned into new deserts of Owens Valley.
Profiteers try to capture what will only evaporate
through their fingers.

Mother Nature's water table has a seat for all.

This water, it trickles down our throat
a cold path in the dry heat fast
our life is watered, again.

FULL MOON
CHAPTER 3

The middle ten days of Ramadan are to seek forgiveness.

FIREWORKS

Driving through
our suburban ghetto
in diminishing post-Maghreb afterglow
it sounds like a battlefield.
We jump
as a white-lit rocket
sparkles into the sky to the right
Boom goes a hidden explosion
behind that tree,
Squeee we hear distantly
as the sky glows
and turns black again.
Alert,
unsure of where the next
land mine will hit.
We drive on vigilant.
The horizon is dotted
with explosions –
Jade Flowers
Cherry Bombs
Purple Rain –
kissing the stars with shattered petals on fire
as far as the eyes can see.
On freeways we fly
into the desert night skies
weaving between firecrackers buzzing by
exploding so close
we could reach out
fingers sweeping through flames.

Under the cover of the sulfur smoke
as the ember rains down
my sisters and I
silently we drive on through
vigilant.
Vigilante.

CHAI/LOVER/LOVE

I just want a chai
        that tastes of comfort
        love lingering on lips
        a kiss of sweetness
        that fills my soul with warmth
            a desire to be held
                like I'm home.

I just want a lover
        that tastes of comfort
        love lingering on lips
        a kiss of sweetness
        that fills my soul with warmth
            a desire to be held
                like I'm home.

I once experienced a love
        that tasted of comfort
        a love that lingered on lips
        kisses of sweetness
        that filled my soul with warmth
            a love that held me like I was home.

IFTAR STREETS

In the City of Angels
where driving into the setting sun
under the tall shadows of the desert palm fronds
is this city's absolute icon,
people pray to pavements
giving duas of Road Rage
in cars rushing through
the arteries that give life to this city.
The pink horizon calls my azaan.
With my left hand on the steering wheel
my teeth cut into the sweet date
as my right foot steps on the gas pedal speeding for more.
I should pull over, I think to myself
but in a city where God is invoked in cars, primarily
the wide sky is the dome of my mosque
these roads my prayer rug.
So.
I
Drive
On.

POST-MODERN PRAY

The static-y call of azaan
echoing out the
plastic gold painted mosque
resting on the coffee table –

The grease stains on the
cardboard iftar to-go boxes with
paper napkin wrapped dates and
a pronged spork –

The "Allah is Great" bumper sticker
stuck to the cash register at the
Bangladeshi buffet
in Little Bangladesh –

The cassette tapes playing on
rusty boom boxes
serenading suras mixed with the sounds of
the click-click of plastic zikr beads –

The food splattered photocopied paper
of daily prayer times
stuck with magnets to the
photo covered refrigerator.

HOW WE LOVE

It's dark and
my suhoor of sleep
is cut by the sing-songy sound of
Wake up! It's time to eat!

I'm transported to childhood
where hall lights turn on at 4 am
Ammu's voice would call out
and bowls of frosted flakes would overflow
family would sit at dining table silently eating
till it was time to slumber again.
But I'm grown now, I remember
her voice just a memory echo.

I peek eyes open
to see my non-Muslim BFF houseguest
with a flashlight in one hand
a jug of water in another
It's time to eat! I set my alarm for you!

And I'm reminded
How *khao, khao, khao* means
I love you.
Feeding is how we show love.
Ammu would have been proud.

SURRENDERING TO MY JOY

If we are surrendering witnessing, power, knowledge, and
energy
then let me surrender my giggles to your upturned palms.
Since they say that joy is a radical act of resistance
catch my laughs as if they bubble sacred,
let them fly far and wide.
This joy isn't cavalier.
It can't be when we are laughing in the face of danger –
It's our action of preservation.
It is wholly and uniquely mine. And uniquely yours.
Our joy together will be loud, boisterous,
vibrate us into the future.
One day at a time.

MOON TIME

The moon is tied to the womb
The womb tides with
The pull of the moon
My womb tides,
So in tune with how
The moon forces pull a tide
Our womb gives tithes
To the moon
Waves give tidings
Our body dances tidal waves
My body gravitates to the moon
The way she gravitates back to her.

FLYING THROUGH SUNSET

When flying into the sunset
at what time do I break my fast?
Do I follow the moon as she chases the sun
waiting for a glimpse of fading light?
Is it the flash of green light at the mid-air horizon
or the glimmer of the first star in the sky?
Does it happen at the exact point where the airplane
pierces the pink sorbet skies?
When time stands still while time traveling
through outer space of the Maghreb
where lies the intersection?
It is here that frozen split second
over clouds in space
refusing to be exempt
hanging on by a celestial
sliver of perpetual horizon
I crave to satiate my fast
but to be liminal in perpetuity.

FROM SEEDS

Is there sadaqah
in snails eating the strawberries
from my garden sprung from my seeds?
Or the doves that eat from the bird feeder
before shitting on my car?
Or the earwigs nesting in last year's bulbs
or the worms rooting through rotting soil?
Learn to be gracious
for your errant charity.

FULL STRAWBERRY MOON

6:10 AM PST Friday June 9th:
The Strawberry Moon is full
telling us we are exactly halfway there.
We've peaked, we've climaxed, we're reaching full
potential.
But have I made the most of the fast so far?
Have I forgiven, prayed, loved enough?

Chani tells us
the full moon is in Sagittarius this Ramadan
and as my rising sign
I've been in rigorous self-development.
And this moon is a catalyst
of meeting an ending with graciousness.

Maybe it's as simple as the fast of the day.
Or maybe it's about the difficult month of Ramadan.
Or maybe it's the people that have hurt my heart.
Or maybe not knowing what my life plans are next.
Or maybe I'm not going to find someone who loves me.
Or maybe I'll never have a child of my own.

I fast hard this Jummah day
waiting for the flower moon to
bloom in the night sky.
Go through the motions
try to do more, harder.
Wisdom is there on the edge
and we are halfway there.

FULL CAPRICORN MOON

The pink full moon is in Capricorn
peeking over desert edges and motel roofs
from behind wispy gray clouds
between silhouettes of dark palms.
She rises slow into the deep 122-degree heat
shining a purple pastel on the world.
She tells us to have faith in the process
and to purge what cannot support us in the long-run.
From the tall fronds a deep buzzing persists
the cicadas are in choir running songs into each other.
In the morning, dried raindrops in desert dirt pepper
outside –
overnight, the Capricorn skies cried.

MAKING WITCHY DUAS

For Randa Jarrar

At the café
over my jinn scar she stood
muttering Islamic incantations
spells from her tongue fell
spreading protection.
Her prayers are infused with the feminization of God
  What do you mean you make Allah linguistically
  feminine?
she brought palo santos infused bismillahs
and is coloring while discussing BDSM with her various
fuckbois
  What do you mean you get men to obey you?
Later, I text her my joy
she says her connection to Allah
is her belief that we can heal each other
Later, I text her my rejection
she says I'm queen, these dudes need to be coming to me
This is the kind of Muslim witchiness I believe in
One brewing in a cauldron of pleasure, pain, healing
Mashallah, I'm placing her poetry
on my altar next to the zamzam water
  is this what joy feels like?
   I had forgotten.

KIRIN'S HEART

For Kirin Khan

the ultrasound shows
your heart upside down and reversed
so, the right ventricle pumps out the wrong side and up.
your heart pounds in pixelated gray
clenching muscle chambers
a storm brewing inside
in blue/red/yellow sonogram bursts of blaze.

even though your hospital gown back is to me and you are
yards away
together we watch your life beat on the screen
searching for secret signs or messages from within
something to tell us why
your body has sabotaged itself.

there is something incredibly intimate
about looking inside your heart
more intimate than reading diary pages or holding hands
or eye contact on a see-saw.
I am seeing you, inside out.

your heart floats in your chest
unattached to your breath, ribs, muscles
you stay still,
and we wonder to ourselves then —
how your heart doesn't fall?
how does our unattached heart not fall?

in this moment, I am your witness
we all need a witness sometimes to our beating hearts
assurance that we are alive and lived.

HAMSA ON RAMY'S RIB

For Ramy El-Etreby

You love so deep
you cracked your ribs
protecting your heart
from assholes.
I imagine
gently pressing my fingers
to your ribcage –
palms cast on bones,
the hamsa of my hand
holding your tender heart in place.
Manifest that love for yourself you deserve
I'll be here for now, a talisman
All these damned evil eyes curved.

BEING HUMAN IS DIVINE

For Jason Chu

Maybe he was right. Maybe the fact I wasn't filled with a magical blessedness from fasting was a myth I was chasing. Maybe this time wasn't meant for that feeling. He said he fasted too, but in a Christian way. And for him, the magic of divinity laid in what was human. What makes us human. The hunger. The loss of focus. The headache. The dryness of skin. The cottonmouth. How the heat radiates and doesn't from your skin. How you feel your body, from the inside out – your heart, your lungs, your blood. The change in natural rise and fall of energy. How all of that sucked and was hard – but it was a reminder we are human. And this was our body. And this is life. And maybe in that reminder that we are human, is that divinity.

That's right, I remind myself. *Being human is divine.*

Maybe I was seeking something that wasn't there to be sought. But rather, divinity was seeking me. And I almost missed it.

MIXED GENDER PRAYER

Al hamdu lillaahi rabbil 'alameen.
We whispered in-sync, in community, in concert.

With palms raised up, faces down and our words sinking
into colorful prayer mats spread wall to wall. Our mixed-
gender Muslim prayer was genderqueer of beautiful
people – cis women standing shoulder to shoulder with gay
men; femme arms brushing trans hands; dark lipsticks and
bright kufis, sparkly hijabs and somber beards. We prayed
for souls lost that night, for solace for everyone feeling
pain, for seeds of love to sprout at ignored intersections.
We appealed to Allah to make this fast easy, to brace us
for bravado, to bless us with the strength to move forward.
Together, our mouths bit into juicy dates to break our
daylong fast. But it's not enough to fill the empty hollow
inside.

So, we continue to whisper,
Ameen Ameen Ameen...

JUMMAH AT THE WOMEN'S MOSQUE

And then maybe, as the muezzin's beautiful voice sang the azaan as only a woman could, reverberating magic through our makeshift mosque, maybe I finally felt compelled to pray. And then maybe, if I had been raised in life to calls of prayer by a woman's voice in a women's space, maybe I would have lived a whole life where I felt actually invited to pray. And then maybe, I'd pray.

MY HEART SINGS

If music is haram
then why does listening to azaan make my heart sing?
If it isn't halal
then why does it sound like a chorus when we all say
ameen?

Suras are sung through recited lips
finger tips dancing on Arabic script
thosbee beads going click, click, click.

Lines are made lyrical
creating a treble to make veins tremble
a bass to make breath breathless
a shiver to center to let nur enter
words so temptress
it makes soul music jealous.

Or maybe it's just the pages of the Quran
are music sheets for the soul
striking like the bangs of a dhol,
true blues in the raw
where faith love is law and
angel wings beat to a tempo
of musical manifesto.
So...

If music is truly haraam
then heart beats would turn to rock
veins frozen into ice blocks
rhythm of life would stop.

Faith wouldn't resonate.
Soul would be sedate.

In my truth,
faith
is sung
with love.

SHE IS HUNGRY

Ramadan sun breaks
Ramadan rage
sidewalk grays glint
as heat pulses on
cold brown skin
during lonesome lunch breaks
she is hungry for heat, warmth, light, touch

BEFORE SUHOOR

For Basim

We talked on the phone through the night
till suhoor beckoned you away
long lost lovers
broken up for years
breaking into a fast
while the devil can't play
insomnia's lust for a love long gone

HALFWAY THERE

Can the full moon see this rage?
Shine a moonbeam of calm
cut through this angered apathy.
My empty belly empties my heart
everything is everything is nothing
my thirstiness un-satiated.
Halfway through and Ramadan is not filling me.
It's just testing me.
Oh Moon, show me other ways to light my life.

ZIKR

Bead, Click, Sweep
bead click sweep
beadclicksweep
Whisper
Allah
Greatness
All Knowing
All Forgiving
sweepclickbead
sweep click bead
Sweep, Click, Bead
Laughter
Allah
Joyful
All Loving
Ecstatically
Sweepclickbead
sweep click bead
Click, Click, Click
Bead
Bead
Bead

TIME FOR SEHRI

Published on Muslim Women Speak

I am deep in slumber when I hear knocks on my bedroom door. "Wake up, it's time sehri!" I hear a voice singsong while my door is timidly opened.

For a moment, while my eyes are closed, I think the voice is my Mom's. I'm in my childhood bedroom in my childhood bed with those childhood plastic stars on my popcorn ceiling. If it had been Mom, she would have left the door open with the light from the hallway spilling into my bedroom. I'd wake up drearily and silently and make my way to kitchen where she would have put a box of Frosted Flakes, milk, and a bowl at my seat of the dining table. Dad would be eating mangos, poha and yogurt. Mom would be standing by the sink eating leftovers. It'd be dark outside. We'd eat quietly. We'd all keep an eye on the clock making sure that we didn't eat through fajr.

"What time is it?" I mumble into my pillow. I put my hand out searching for my phone and try looking at the time through bleary eyes.

"It's 2am! Get up and get ready!" my sister says, both sternly and fake cheerfully.

"It's only 2am! The end of sehri isn't until 4:17am! I just fell asleep at 1am! Why!?" I snuggle my face deeper into my pillow.

"Because we have to drive to Denny's and order food. Hurry up!" she says curt as she walks away.

I turn over and stare at the stars on my ceiling. I remember that I'm at my parents' house for the weekend like I have been for every weekend this Ramadan. My sisters are here too, and I had come home this night so that we could go on a sehri trip to Denny's. I don't know at what point eating diner meals at 3am became a part of our annual Ramadan ritual as sisters. But it had.

My two sisters and I silently make our way out the door to the car. It is dark outside and the neighborhood is lined with silhouettes of California ranch homes. The streets are eerily empty with only streetlamps lighting our deserted way. I think to myself that at 2:30 am, this is usually the time when people at bars come stumbling home and but here we were heading out to eat. Only religion or alcohol would compel people to leave the house this late at night.

We are driving about six houses down from our home when my youngest sister exclaims from the backseat of the car, "Is that a real fire? Should we do something?" I look up and to my right. There's an orange glow behind a fence, and as I look longer, a red blaze leaps up 10 feet high, silhouetted by the outline of white roof. The fire looks like it's between two houses, or maybe it's the backyard of another house. The fear makes ups all wake up instantly.

My other sister backs the car so that we can get a better view. It looks like a fire that just started, but it was big and growing quick. There's no way that flame was from a backyard barbecue. We can see now that we are looking at the back of a house on the other side of the block. I look around – there is not another car on the road, the lights on the houses are off, and no one is around. I jump out of the car as my youngest sister calls 911. I run up to the house with the American flag and bang on the metal door. "The

house behind you is on fire!" I say to the man who opens
the door. He is an older larger middle-aged white man. He
says, that he just woke up and he knows and he disappears
back in the house.

There are now a couple of other cars have stopped by ours
and a few neighbors come out to the sidewalk to stand by
us. A guy in a big red truck tells us that he had driven by
the house on fire on the other side - the man had gotten
out safely, but couldn't ask much else since he spoke
another language.

I go to the next house in the path of the embers and knock
on the door – but they ignore my knocks. I know that they
are in there because the window blinds are parted. My
youngest sister goes back to the that house a few minutes
later – she talks to a teenage Filipino girl who is taking
care of her elderly grandparents. She listens to my sister.
We see the granddaughter struggle in evacuating her
grandparents – one of them needs a wheelchair - but they
are moving too slowly. So my sister goes inside to help
the Lola find her keys – she finds 5 sets of keychains and
throws them all in the bag before helping the Lola out.

With nothing left to do, my sisters and I stand on the
sidewalk as we watch the house go up in flames. It is
clearer now that we are looking at the back of the house
between two houses and behind a fence – and that a back
bedroom was the origin of the fire. The fire moves like a
slow creature across the house, it creeps into the attic and
flames slowly lick out of the various windows. We gasp
as fire bursts through cracks in the eaves of the roof. We
clutch our hearts – it looks like the flames are alive.

The fire is deadly quiet.

When you watch fires on television or in person when you are sitting around a campfire, there is a sound to the fire – you can hear the crackling of the wood or crunch of the lumber. Fires are devastating and loud. We are shaking - how could a burning house come apart so quietly? As we stand watching, you can hear the night birds chirping in the trees. The streets are still eerily silent.

The fire trucks pull into our neighborhood without sirens – we see their blinking red and orange lights behind the growing smoke. It took them 15 minutes to get there – by then, it seems the whole house is engulfed. We hear the chainsaw as they cut holes into the attic. We see the spray of water and a column of smoke rise. We look onward with fear as embers fly onto the houses we had just evacuated. We stand there until the last flame has disappeared, as if our mere presence could have served to fight against lingering embers. By the end, everything was singed.

I kept thinking about how if we had left the house later, we wouldn't have been there in time to call 911. Would there have been anyone else on the road to see it? Or what if we had decided to do our sehri diner tradition on a Saturday instead of a Friday? And what were the chances that the one night of the whole month of Ramadan that I leave the house for sehri, that this should even happen? They say it is sunnah to eat food at sehri – but not obligatory in Islam – what if we had simply made the choice to not eat sehri? What opportunity had presented itself in this moment? Was this a sign from Allah of some sort? Or was it just an ordinary miracle?

We get back in the car and debate continuing our trip to Denny's – it feels a bit disrespectful to the soberness of the moment but our adrenaline is ramped up way too high

for any of us to go to sleep. It is only 3am and we still have
another hour to eat. While we eat pancakes at Denny's,
we see a Muslim family walk-in – the parents are in their
30s and the three young boys are rambunctious. They are
sitting too far to say salaams, but it is warming to know we
were sharing the same meal. I think about how these sehri
trips to Denny's will become a part of the little boys' future
nostalgia.

On our way home, we drive by the street where the burnt
house is. The street is covered with fire trucks and it is
impossible to drive through. We turn the car around and
go home for last minute gulps of water. We laugh as we
fight to fill our glasses and drink the water quick. We enter
restless sleep. I find comfort in knowing that my sisters
tonight sleep in the same house as me.

I keep thinking about the man who didn't speak English
whose house was burned down. Did he have fire
insurance? Sure, he was alive, but would he be okay? Was
he alone? Would Allah provide for him?

Ramadan is supposed to be a month of reflection, prayer,
and fasting. But here we are at the end of the month, and
I am not sure that I "got" anything out of it. This year,
fasting brought my rage closer to the surface, and I found
myself unable to get spiritually grounded. My Muslim-ness
was often performative as I read poetry on stages and
hosted activist-y events, but where was the heart in it all.
I fasted every day that I could this Ramadan. But I didn't
go to the mosque, I often broke fasts solo, I didn't keep
all my prayers and didn't write as much as I had intended
to. I was searching for that spirituality clicking that feels
so centering this time of the month that just didn't happen
this time. And, I think, that I had been unconsciously asking

for a sign. A burning house at sehri time sure feels like a sign.

I had forgotten. Ramadan is about empathy, and giving, and the humanity of all. I had forgotten it is about charity and giving back to your community. I had forgotten that this life we lead is temporary, and life can change in an instant, and we have no control. I had forgotten that we needed to find joy in our everyday life because life is indeed fleeting. We must find joy and humanity whenever possible. That finding joy in hardship is a form of radical resistance and that is a form of worship.

I drive by the house the next day. Besides the plywood on the front door and front window, and some black soot along the eaves, from the front of the house it looks like a fire hardly touched it. I am shocked that something that had seemed so tragic could have left such little echoes of its presence.

May we all have the humanity to always step up when we are called.

May this be a Ramadan lesson for us all.

Eid Mubarak.

WANING CRESCENT
CHAPTER 4

The last ten days of Ramadan are to seek safety, from hell and otherwise.

THIRSTING

I drink all night till almost the break of dawn
but satiating my dehydration
only makes my slumbered cravings stronger.
It's as if fasting reminds my body what else it is missing.

Instead of longing for water
I throw myself deep into my sleep.
These Ramadan dreams are full of thirst
lustful naps pulling me into different illusive arms
leaving my throat parched
my lips chapped
a body so shook
I wonder if I broke my fast in my dreams.

TIME PASS FOR PEOPLE LIKE ME

We measure days with slivers of moons
and not the setting suns
We measure space with quiet longing
and not close distance
We measure life with weeds on graves
and not baby hairs
We measure time with fasting hunger pangs
not gorged on wedding buffets
We measure desire with desert night drives
not honeymoon suites
We measure lust with bedpost notches
not morning after eggs
We measure love with lonesome
not oxytocin
We measure heartache with needles in chest graveyards
not shedding of warm tears
We measure heartbeats with calloused fingers
not calloused kisses

We measure infinity with future breaths and past regrets.
We travel through time in measures of
soul rhythms unlike the rest.

PRE/AY

When I am their prey
is when I pray the most.
To not be preyed for how I pray
and that these prayers will hold me safe,
      Prayed upon
       instead of preyed on –
          so, let us pray.

MAKE A WISH ON A SHOOTING JINN

I saw a light
falling from the night sky
streaking shimmering green.
I couldn't decide
if I was supposed to avert my eyes from a falling jinn
or make a wish upon a shooting star.
Glowing brighter
it trailed into the downtown lights.
If the gates of hell were closed for Ramadan,
where does the jinn rejected from heaven's gates fall?
It bursts into imploded oblivion
leaving nothing but black skies
shadows on my retina.
Was it too late to make a wish?
Would the jinn find me to be able to grant it?
Did I see what I just saw?
And just like that,
the darkness of night descends, again.

HAZE

Today
Los Angeles smells like India,
Like heavy fog and survival trash burning
Like the thick air
Of dawn and dusk
With almost humidity
And almost dreams
And almost warm at road sides.
It smells dirty
Like struggle
Like life in every suck of breath.
Lungs choke with each deep inhale.
Muscle memories in vertigo
Unsure of where I'm placed.
This smell
Always confusing me with a longing for home
When home is where I stay at.
Here, home is
Smog tinged horizons in hazy yellows and smoky pinks.
Only LA's pollution tinged coastal sunsets
Have 4th dimension colors of epic.
But there,
Smoke us the smell of home
Of azaan at fajir
And sweaty cold sheets,
Dust coating everything
And trash gets burned for struggled warmth
And death gets burned for serenity in eternity
And here
Smoke is the smell of survival

So maybe
Survival is my solace.
And maybe why the smell of moist smoke is home.

WHIRLING DERVISH OF A JINN

My back was on fire as jinns howled ferociously in the wind
a swirled burn scar on my left shoulder blade to prove it
the scream of pain before I saw the flames.
This is not a metaphor.
My back sears with punishment
from talking about jinns during Maghreb windstorms
when the acupuncturist cupped me with fire and glass.
It was no coincidence
to catch on fire right then.
I knew it was but the psychic confirmed it
as her eyes lit with glee.
This must look very strange to you, to see me laugh, she said.
But I see a whirling spinning jinn dancing on your back.
It's gone now.
Ammu was right all along –
Jinns do fly at Maghreb time.
This is a fact.

BLEEDING

Are you on vacation?
the auntie whispers salaciously
as if the blood dripping
out of my pussy is a
dark dirty shameful secret
meant to fill me with regret.
This blood is unholy.
It is a gift from God.
What do you mean, my PERIOD?
I respond deadpan.
She looks appalled.
I take a sip of water.
Finally, I'm able to think again.
This body is alive
I am reminded.

RHAPSODOMANCY

*Rhapsodomancy is an ancient form of divination
performed by choosing through some method a specific
passage or poem from which to ascertain information.*

**

Rhapsodomancy
with Spotify Shuffle
his lyrics divination
to manifest my divine.
Oh Spotify,
point out in his shuffled album of thine
all I have to do.

But what about when he finally kissed me?
Shuffle // Play
>   *You take me back to bad ideas*, he croons.

But what if I just miss being touched by a man?
Shuffle // Play
>   *They screamed at her, don't turn back*, he lilts.

But what about how my heart skips beats, again?
Shuffle // Play
>   *Tom tom*, he sings.

But what if my heart squeezes with rejection?
Shuffle//Play
>   *I picked up all the purple you dropped*, he sings.

But what if it wasn't chasing love, but chasing to be seen?
Shuffle // Play
> *It's a little too late, it's a little too late*, he
> serenades.

The songs shuffle and play
on and on
It was divined from his lips to Allah's ears
in his very own lyrics
anyways
I can't claim
I hadn't heard
already.

I WILL PRAY WHERE I WANT

Texas skies are so big when it's Maghreb time, it feels like you've been swallowed whole into a pink sorbet fantasy with an endless horizon.

Listen to how pretty the birds sing in that tree, Abbu, I say as he walks up the sidewalk corner.

It sounds like a hundred swallows are greeting the night skies. I say it overly casually, like standing on sidewalk corners at sunset listening to birds in trees is my normal activity.

I say it like I wasn't side-eyeing on one side each White Man walking out of cars with big wheels and trump stickers and on the other side keeping an eye on dad praying Maghreb in his parked car.

I say it like I wasn't clench fisted and practicing self-defense moves in my heard and turning retorts on my tongue. I say it so he doesn't feel like I am watching him, challenging his masculinity, his elderliness, his ego. I say it so he doesn't feel watched by not just one but the other.

This isn't shame or infantilizing, I want him to understand – *it's not you, it's everyone else* – I want to echo back the words he'd scream at the teenage version of me.

But instead I say, *I think they are swallows, I think, singing.*

The bird is singing?

I think it's more than one singing, Abbu. And yes, they are singing.

The next day at the airport, when I tell him I'll see if they have a prayer room, he rages.

Why do you always have to be like that, he fumes. I will pray where I want.

I looked hard, but couldn't find any singing sparrows inside the airport that day.

FORGIVE AND FORGET

I learned young
how to lock the bathroom door behind me
with my back pushing on it with all my little strength
I learned quickly
to find safety in the hiding places of the dark recesses of
closets
how to hold my heaving breath still as I cried quietly
I learned early
to hide the wooden dowels and hangers that appeared in
corners
how to curl my spine to keep the welts to my back and my
arms raised protect my face
I never learned
how to predict the rage
how to know what set him off
how to keep from triggering his hot temper
I never learned
how to be the obedient daughter
how to respect a man that never earned it
how to trust anyone but myself
and I never learned
how in his old age, how I'm supposed to forgive this man
for things he denies and no longer remembers
I never understood why all this was so easy
for him to forget
because
if he doesn't remember...
how can I forgive
and forget?

GOUT

If pink crystals are supposed to be filled with the energetic energies of love and violet crystals bring you intuition and dreams, then I wonder what color the crystals growing inside my father must be. Maybe sky black like the rage in his eye, or blood red like his hot temper. In reality it's probable the crystals are gray, tired, and fragile. My father is so old he is a geode growing crystals on his bones. His kidney is a glass factory crystalizing his cave. His joints crackle with what his body is unable to process. From the inside out, his body is turning into stone.

With crystal balls you can see the future and with crystal wands you can send energy into the grid around this world. With crystal innards can you see the poisons of the past? Can energy be re-aligned from the inside out when crystalizing from the inside out?

When this geode cracks, will it be magic or will it all just simply be dust... only Allah knows.

FWD: TXT

Today dad texted,
Last 10 days of Ramadan
for forgiveness
make sure you ask Allah
to forgive you
and your Mom
and Dad
and Sisters.
And I wondered
in the subtext
just Who
was asking Who
for forgiveness
and Who
it was presumed
had sinned.

ARE YOU THERE, GOD?

In a circle of friends, we sat with palms in the air, on bed sheets of stopgap prayer rugs. Each one us took turns making duas for something grand, for something blessed, for something grateful. We took turns for these duas. We affirmed with ameens. We affirmed loudly so the angels would ameen in-sync.

Duas were made for compassion, for social justice, for appreciation of community. Duas were made for babies and laughter, for reminders that we are loved. Duas were made for blessings to keep us from straying from the paths, duas were made for love in all of its deconstructed ways.

When it was my turn, I froze. I was out of practice. And I can't tell if I've forgotten or if I've just never really learned how to pray from my heart. Or maybe I was truly self-sufficiently ungrateful. Or scared. Conversation is a two-way street but I was raised to dogmatically cower in Arabic. Fear was never a respectful conversation starter. Stunned, I thought to myself, it's no wonder my prayers have never been heard.

So, I said "ditto". And then I said, "ameen".
And everyone else echoed with "ameens"
And I asked myself, what am I actually praying for anyways?
How do I decolonize my duas anyways?

THE WAR INSIDE US ALL

If the gates of hell are closed
shaitan is shackled
this madness
in the death and destruction
that we see now
then how naturally evil
actually
is at the core
of our humanity?

HATE CRIMES

I stepped out of my car, pink skies streaking dusky blues overhead. The hot desert heat stung my skin while the temperature simultaneously dropped dramatically, stirring up that Maghrib winds that conjures up images of swooping invisible jinns snatching at your uncovered hair. Apprehensively I stood, looking first at the large American flag gracing the chain linked fence of the house across the street. I then looked at the mosque, which was really just a 1970s California ranch style house that was being used as a mosque – the Al Nur Mosque located in Ontario, California. It was hard to think that this was the "scary Mozlem temple" that elicited three pig feet being thrown in the driveway only days earlier by two women in a white truck during the sacred late-night Ramadan prayers.

Last time I had been in a mosque was last year when my mother had died, and the last time I had been in this mosque was for the special prayer we held 48 hours after her burial. It was the most spiritually connected moment of my life. I hadn't been that connected since then, and it held me paralyzed as I stood breathlessly by my car. I wondered how I'd be accepted in this space, showing up alone without my Mom by my side. She was my community conduit. The mosque was created and attended by the Bangladeshi immigrant community that raised me but I was an adult now and building my own communities. But the events of the week weighed down terribly on me, and I knew that I had to be present in this particular mosque as a show of solidarity – or maybe more as a statement. I practiced my Islam defiantly, wore my religion on my brown skin politically. I was Muslim, despite America's fear.

I stepped into the backyard. I was greeted by foldable
tables lined up in rows, paper tablecloths whipping in the
wind. The tables were covered with plates of pakoras,
channa, and dates, glasses of rose flavored pink drink. Men
in white kurtas and thupees sat on one side of the yard,
women with dupattas wrapped around their heads sat on
the other. The imam caught my eye and smiled at me in
recognition. I meekly smiled back. Last time I had seen him
we had gotten into a fight over my insistence of having the
women's prayer section up front next to the men's section
for Mom's funeral prayer instead of hidden in a back room.
My Islam was radical in that way.

The mood was calm, normal even. There was no fear
hanging in the air, nor were there giddy pleasantries. It felt
placid. People saw me and nodded wordlessly, as if after all
these years, they'd been expecting me.

It had been a long hot day of 109 degrees and people
were ready to break their fast. Somewhere in the house,
the imam began azaan and the call for prayer. Dates were
eaten, water sipped. The tables emptied quietly as people
filtered in to pray and as if on cue the desert wind kicked
up, knocking pink drinks all over the paper lined tables.
The calm mood struck me as odd but in made sense given
the context. If there's something you learn from a day of
fasting in long and hot weather, it's that you have no time
for bullshit.

I, on the other hand, was festering from the weight of the
Islamophobia of the week.

On the first few days of August in Oakland, California,
several South Asian organizers commenced the *Bay Area
Solidarity Summer* for the second year, a 4-day long

camp on South Asian American activism for South Asian American teenagers. I was excited to share knowledge with the twelve youth that were attending this year. The first piece I had a role in was a curriculum that involved timelining the legacy of South Asian American history, connecting their personal activism with the legacy of South Asian American unheard history of activism.

The second was a workshop on Islamophobia that we conducted on Saturday night. Our curriculum walked them through Islamophobic microaggressions cases to larger systematic forms of oppression and state violence, and then finally, closing with tools to combat and resist. With about 75% of the youth being non-Muslims, our biggest concern with the workshop was emphasizing the need for pan South Asian solidarity when it comes to being racialized as "Brown" in America and how Islamophobia wasn't just a Muslim issue, but affected all communities of color. After a couple of hours of images, stats and sharing various tools of resistance, we did a "group check-in" to see what tools the youth would take back with them to their community. Some said they would take what they learned back to student organizations on their campus, build alliances with Muslim groups and have conversations with their family members. I thought the Islamophobia workshop had been a success, when one of the participants stated, "This is great – but it doesn't affect my community. I don't have to worry about this."

I was stunned because it was clear that as we had moved along through our narrative, we had missed this participant for some reason. Other participants spoke up, providing peer-to-peer insight and group dialogue. I wondered what we trainers could have done differently that would have worked and would have convinced this youth that

Islamophobic terror was alive and well and needed
solidarity, even by non-Muslims. And then we woke up
Sunday morning to the devastating shooting at the Sikh
Gurudwara in Oak Tree, Wisconsin. It is what they call a
"teachable moment", I guess.

It was I that broke the news of the shooting to our youth,
after they came back from a community walk. I framed it in
the context of the Islamophobia workshop from the night
before. Their faces slackened; eyes went to the ground.
We had a moment of silence. We kept open space for
dialogue, if they wanted. They didn't. We moved on in the
curriculum, circling back to the event throughout the rest
of the weekend.

I hated doing that.

I hate that to train our youth to be activists and leaders,
we need to teach them about the hate in the world and
how they will be hated for things beyond their control. I
hate how quickly and easily a real-world example fell into
our laps after a tough workshop on concepts that go above
most people's heads. I hate that it had been over ten years
since September 11th and that we are not done with this
– and instead of backlash, fear of "the other Brown" is
now intrinsically systematic within our society and media,
with seven foundations having funding $42 million of
islamophobic hate. I hate that feeling that four days wasn't
enough for the BASS training and that we didn't give our
youth enough tools, or education, or love to counter all the
hate they will face as future organizers.

At the closing circle for BASS, each youth grabbed an image
from the South Asian Legacy timeline, and shared why they
were taking back that particular image with them. It was

hard to close the safe and loving space we had created for our team of organizers and participants, knowing what was out there in the real world. As I drove down the I-5 away from Oakland back home to Los Angeles, I prayed that we had equipped our BASS youth with enough love and fire to face this grief filled unjust world as fighters and with bravado. *Ameen.*

In the days since the shooting and BASS, the events haven't stopped. It is almost as if the white supremacists saw what happened in Wisconsin and were empowered even further to act out. In the past 11 days the South Asian community has been the recipient of eight attacks, and counting. A mosque in Missouri was burned to the ground. Shots were fired from a pellet rifle at the wall of a mosque in Chicago. Nearby, a soda bottle full of acid was flung at an Islamic school. In Rhode Island, a man head butted and pulled down a sign in front of a mosque and in Hayward, teens were caught pelting oranges and lemons at mosque attendees.

The incident in Ontario, California was minimal in comparison, though just as chilling. The small Bangladeshi community in the Inland Empire started meeting monthly in living rooms in the mid-90s. At the time, the mosques in the area were dominated by Pakistani and Arabs and there wasn't a Bangladeshi space to pray. By the late 90s they had moved to an office space in a strip mall, across the street from a sex toy shop. They've since moved twice, this last time to a ranch house they bought tucked in the unincorporated part of the town. They've been raising money for years, with the hopes of building a mosque on the land the ranch house is on. But the neighbors have not been happy with this move and have been fighting every step of the way. The mosque has notices taped on the inside wall, letters from inspectors, that show that the congregation is not illegal as long as there are less than 500 people and that they have all the right permits in place.

As people met nightly for the daily taraweeh prayers in Ramadan, they saw women taking pictures of the mosque. They wouldn't disclose their names when asked. A few days later, a white truck with two women was parked suspiciously in front of the mosque. Wary, the mosque hired a security guard. That very night, the white truck came back and two women dropped three pig feet on the driveway of the mosque at 10pm. The congregation finished their prayer, and when they were done around 11pm, they picked up the feet and threw them in the trash. They called up the San Bernardino's Sherriff's Department and are requesting that a full investigation be made and for this to be reported as a hate incident. Everyone came back to pray the very next day.

When I was at the mosque this weekend, I was comforted by the sound of Arabic prayers lilting through the dusky heat. There was something about it that reminded me of being home. I was a little taken aback, when I came to that realization. In a way this was home. This was the mosque I was raised in, these were the community members that saw me grow from a child to an adult and this was the community that helped bury my mother with all the beautiful Muslim rituals that escaped me only the year before. All the aunties shared sweet Ramadan memories of praying side by side with my mother. Here I was home in Islam, where I didn't need to be defiantly Muslim after being subjected to othering - I had nothing to prove to anyone here. This was a community of folks that simply wanted to meet and pray together. Build a space where they could take care of each other. No political statement.

Just spiritual and community.

I realized this weekend that with all my organizing
and activism that maybe the real revolutionaries
were immigrants of our parents' generation - building
community with Islam and creating places of worship
despite all the fear and racialization and otherizing put on
them in this new world.

Solidarity is needed now more than ever before. We are
four days away from Eid, a month away from September
11th and 3 months away from Election Day. Islamophobia
escalates around these key days. As isolated events, the
events of the week were intimidating – but as a collection
of events, it is reflective of the systematic oppression that
is fueled by the right wing Islamophobia machine. We must
stand together to counter these actions. We must push
the mainstream media and policymakers to bring light to
these stories. We must all visit mosques and gurudwaras
and have interfaith dialogue. And we as a South Asian
community, we need to continue to educate and our new
generation about legacy, building unity and real solidarity.

The name of the mosque is Al Nur which translates into a
pure and godly inner light. Kind of fitting, I think. Let's keep
shining on.

EID AL-FITR
CHAPTER 5

Eid begins the day (beginning at sunset) of the first sighting of the crescent moon shortly after sunset. The next three days are for celebration.

SPEAK

Say *ameen*
For when humanity teeters on morality
For when dreams question your reality
For when heart breaks in old crackled patterns
For solitude's inward shatters
Say *ameen*
For the illogical manifesting into the norm
For the relativity of free thought deformed
Say *ameen*
To uncertainty / to failures / to risks
Say *ameen*
To disharmony / to fractures / to conflicts
Say *ameen*
Because you are still alive
In this fucked up world
You still have the will and courage to survive
Say *ameen*
For when you can't say anymore
Say *ameen*
When there's no words to answer for

JUST ONE DAY

I just want a day
where I can relish in all of the beauty of God
– the miracles of the moon,
or the beauty of the flower fields,
or the joy and pleasure of being alive –
instead of the belief of said god
in this skin
placing a target on my back
that I'm running back and forth constantly to dodge.

FUTURE PAGES

What of this future is to be foretold
with the bibliomancy of
the blank pages in this empty notebook?
shadows of butterfly dreams
distant echoes of skipped heart beats
words better left unsaid
missed connections best not unearthed
lost lovers never found
potential lovers disinterested
weighted silence of nothingness
the limit to your imagination
forgotten prayers
perpetuity of lonely
unshed tears
emptiness
What are you waiting for;
the future awaits.

BEHIND THE PURDAH

Oh Moon,
where are you tonight
on this dry desert
of sleepy lights?
Remove your purdah of darkness
shine us your sliver
anew.
Tell us
is the grace of Ramadan
over?

MOON WAX

Driving west
chasing the moon sliver
hanging over the hills on the horizon.
Maghreb darkens into night.
A new moon, a waxing crescent.
It must be Eid.
It is over.

Look at how she smiles. Slyly.
Like she knows how shaitan has
been released from heaven's chains.
From her cosmic perch
she sees the world unraveling.
She smirks, wryly.
I drive on, following her into the darkness.
The moon is the beacon I can't escape.
Ramadan is done.

SPOTTED ON THE RADAR

A ladybug bloom
a mile high
across the desert
lit by a crescent waxing
a green cloud on weather radars
an omen
a symbol of something
a night where heaven's gates are open
Ramadan wishes sent skyward
prayers soaring through celestial space
a celebration
a government cover-up
a mystical maybe
a devil freed
a congregation of Eid dreams
a hoard of lady luck of ladybugs –
As we sleep
our Eid-ie dreams
overhead the red beetles bloom symbolically
telling us something we were not to know.

CALCULATING SMILE

We chased her cross the fading sky
searching for a sliver from east to west
squinting through telescopes on mountain tops
coaxing her from cavernous night darkness
waiting for calls from this imam or texts from that mosque
seeking a witness of her elusive sly smile.
Astronomy tells us she is visible for twenty-six minutes
after sunset in Los Angeles,
but no naked eye on the horizon
can see it through this June Gloom Haze
cartographers map us in real time on moonsighting.com
documenting worldwide as she drifts in her orbit
listing Fullerton, CA where she is caught briefly, first.
This must be what they mean by "calculations"
but still, people climb to hilltops,
the local masjid says tomorrow and the Shurrah Council
says day after
but what do the Wahabis of Mecca say?

She keeps moving with her calculating sly smile across the
night sky
as if she knows only the exact moment with shaitan
chained up.
And we people wonder when exactly we can begin.

COTTONMOUTH CANDY SKIES

Ramadan ends at sunset
with cotton candy skies
bittersweet
tastes like the end
the finish of a month
of fasting so delicious
the start of thirst, un-satiated
it is a split-second moment
when the skies open
the sunset and your gut wrenches
with the knowledge
of not accomplishing
half the things wished for
and knowing there will be
twice the prayers waiting till next year.
This is the feeling of
missing it before it's over
colliding with now
cotton candy stuffs your mouth
this bitterness is hard to swallow
without the sweetness of future.

EID PRAYERS

They armored themselves in the finest garb – rainbow colored anarkalis skimming the ground. Finely embroidered thopis covering their heads. Dupattas of glitter flying in the wind behind. They strapped themselves with strands of lace and pearls. Their wrists were wrapped in gemstone thosbees. They steeled themselves in filigree of gold.

They marched into the prayer hall, hundreds, nay thousands, with only a prayer mat under their arms and armed with not much more. They stood in lines, side-by-side. Words were the only weapons to be brandished at this battle. Prayers were the only battle-cry to be heard.

Were they naïve? Or were they brave? Nightly, people had died – by bullets and by beatings. Nightly, people died from hate and terror. For being who they were. For believing the way they do. They were just pawns, victimized from two sides.

But in this prayer hall, at this Eid prayer, they marched in with pride. Joy flirted on their lips. With heads held high, their jubilant bravado was brazened. They could have been shot. They could have been bombed. They could have not shown up. They could have prayed from home. They could have been scared.

Their celebration was defiant. Or maybe they didn't know better because this was the only way they knew how to behave. Maybe defiance was the default because that was all they had ever known.

HAPPINESS

Today is the day to be happy
the Imam khutbah-ed at Eid prayer
as if 'happiness' were a choice
and 'pleasure' was a form of worship.

The congregation wept
- with joy -
they had held their breath for so long
that they had forgotten why
a weight had been lifted
a collective exhale released
permission given for something
they had forgotten to request in Ramadan's duas.

Life is temporal and
This reality isn't really real
the Imam said choking through tears
and quoting Pharrell -
So, celebrate. Be happy.

GIVE YOUR SALAAMS

My mother told me never to touch another person's feet. I was not supposed to step on books with my feet, or sit on ground pointing my feet to the Holy City. I was supposed to take my shoes off when I entered a home.

I was never supposed to bow down and be subservient to another human being.

It was a Hindu cultural holdover, an un-Islamic Bangladeshi practice. This may have been a cultural custom, but in our home, it wasn't our faith. At dawats, when elders would look at me disdainfully expectantly, I'd stare them down defiantly, standing my ground. I didn't have to – my parents said so – I was taught to bow down to no one. No one but the Almighty.

It was surprising, then, to see my 50-something year old mother crouch down to her 80-something year old father's toes, before she left back for America.

Her right hand reached out to the space below his cotton lungi and gnarly toes. She motioned his feet to her mouth to her heart.
His feet to her mouth to her heart.
His feet to her mouth to her heart.
Her cheeks, to wipe away her tears.

Nana, with his wrinkled shaky right hand lightly touched the crown of her head.
Khandhou nah.
Don't cry.

He grabbed her shoulders, and she got up. Eyes turned
down.

Awkward hugs given, she waved good-bye wildly as she
disappeared through the Kathmandu airport gate. She left
me behind with Nana, to take care of him for one more
week. It was surprising to see Mom practice something
she told me I never had to.

Respect is earned, never blindly given.
Culture is home is faith is love is practice.

That was the last time they would both see each other
alive, ever. It was their last worldly touch of each other.
They are both gone now.

Sometimes though, usually during a California sunset, I
will feel a breeze tickling at my feet, licking at my ankles.
I smile, thinking it's just Ammu stopping by to give her
salaams.

From feet to mouth to heart.

NOTES

Almost all of the poems found in this collection were written during the month of Ramadan over the span of ten years.

"Iftar Streets" & "Haze", *Coiled Serpent; Poets Arising from the Cultural Quakes & Shifts of Los Angeles*, Tia Chucha Press (2016)

"My Heart Sings", *Totally Radical Muslims Zine*, Alliance Of South Asians Taking Action (2015)

"Time for Sehri", Muslim Women Speak https://medium.com/muslim-women-speak/time-for-sehri-7eacae6d2d50 (June 14, 2018)

"Hate Crimes", Racialicious.com (August 15, 2012)

ACKNOWLEDGEMENTS

I give thanks to Allah, I give thanks to poetry, I give thanks to Allah for allowing me to connect with Her through poetry.

One of my last memories of my Mom is her telling me to never stop writing. Writing through my grief to heal was the reason why I wrote in this past decade. Thank you Mom for being the source of inspiration for this project. Thank you family for letting me share my words.

This collection is a work of passion, discovery, and giving myself into a process where the only objective was to create. It was my community of fellow Poetry-A-Day poets that held me accountable to my writing, and exploration of spirituality that allowed me to find myself through words, again. Thank you to all my friends in this group – Muslim, Muslimish and Muslim adjacent: Faisal Mohyuddin, Kirin Khan, Ramy El-Etreby, Sasha Ali, Naazneen Diwan, Sagirah Shahid, Nesima Aberra, Saima Husain, Amanda Quraishi, Amina Shafi Rogers, Zohra Saed, Matheen Siddiqui, Wazina Zondon, Calvin Williams, Nafisa Isa, Asim Rehman, Zuha Khan, Tom Earl, Afrose Ahmed, Jordan Alam, Affad Shaikh, Nasia Anam, Nadia Afghani, Azeem Khan, Nadia Ahmad, Serena Lin, Roxana Dhada, Almas Haider, Logan Siler, Deonna Kelli Sayed, Sham E-Ali Nayeem, Karimi Robert, Dustin Craun, Sahar Pirzada, Hari Alluri and many more.

Thank you to the besties that keep me in an inspired state of community – I am so grateful for the spaces we've created for ourselves: Neelanjana Banerjee, Randa Jarrar, Jean Ho, Jenny Yang, Fawzia Mirza, Akhila Ananth, Navneet Grewal, Oiyan Poon, Xiaojing Wang, Sabiha Basrai, Jenn Pae.

Thank you to the friends that sit with me to write – poetry takes a lot of heart, and feels impossible without friends who sit with me to keep me writing. Ahmed Ali Akbar, Nitasha Sawhney, Erin O'Brien, D'Lo, Vivek Mittal, Dimpal Jain, Esther Tseng, Alison De La Cruz.

I am grateful for all the poetry spaces in Southern California that created POC-lead poetic communities that allowed me to feel safe to share my words: Lionlike Mindstate, Sunday Jump, Our Mic, Avenue 50, Tia Chucha Press, Beyond Baroque, and Writ Large Press. My home mic will always be Tuesday Night Café, the first place I felt brave enough to jump on the mic back in 2006. So grateful to Quincy Surasmith, Sean Miura, and traci kato-kiriyama for always including me in this space, and honoring the Asian American poetry voices of Los Angeles.

Thank you to all the poets whose words have touched me.

If so moved, I challenge everyone to continue to write a poetry a day for Ramadan.

ABOUT THE AUTHOR

Tanzila "Taz" Ahmed is a political strategist, storyteller, and artist based in Los Angeles. She creates at the intersection of counternarratives and culture-shifting as a South Asian American Muslim 2nd-gen woman. She's turned out over 500,000 Asian American voters, recorded five years of the award winning Good Muslim Bad Muslim podcast and made #MuslimVDay cards for a decade. Her essays are published in the anthologies, *New Moons*, *Pretty Bitches*, *Whiter*, *Good Girls Marry Doctors*, *Love Inshallah*, and in numerous online publications. She's published poetry collections *Emdash and Ellipses* (2016) & *The Day The Moon Split in Two* (2020), is featured in *Tia Chucha's Coiled Serpent* (2016) and her poetry has been commissioned by the Center for Cultural Power, PolicyLink, the Garment Worker Center, KPCC's Unheard LA, and more. In July 2023, her first solo visual art show *Aunties with Deadly Stare* was exhibited at LA Artcore and her art has been shown in various exhibits including the Eiteljorg Museum of American Indians and Western Art in the *Acts of Faith* exhibit and the Smithsonian APA Center's *H-1B* exhibit. A protest sign she designed for the 2017 Women's March sits in the permanent archives of the Smithsonian Museum of American History.